DR. RAVI BAGARIA'S
THE TOOTHY STORY
ALL ABOUT KIDS TOOTH WITH ACTIVITIES

BLUEROSE PUBLISHERS
India | U.K.

Copyright © Dr Ravi Bagaria 2023

All rights reserved by author. No part of this publication may be reproduced, stored in a retrieval system or transmitted in any form or by any means, electronic, mechanical, photocopying, recording or otherwise, without the prior permission of the author. Although every precaution has been taken to verify the accuracy of the information contained herein, the publisher assumes no responsibility for any errors or omissions. No liability is assumed for damages that may result from the use of information contained within.

BlueRose Publishers takes no responsibility for any damages, losses, or liabilities that may arise from the use or misuse of the information, products, or services provided in this publication.

For permissions requests or inquiries regarding this publication, please contact:

BLUEROSE PUBLISHERS
www.BlueRoseONE.com
info@bluerosepublishers.com
+91 8882 898 898
+4407342408967

ISBN: 978-93-5741-304-6

Cover design: Shivam
Typesetting: Namrata Saini

First Edition: September 2023

CONTENTS

Chapter 1: OOUCH! My Tooth Hurts 1

Chapter 2: My 1st visit to a Dentist 11

Chapter 3: The Treatment begins for a Healthy tooth .. 25

Chapter 4: Time for a Varnish 35

Chapter 5: A Wobbly Tooth 45

Chapter 6: Braces for Kids 55

Fun with Stickers 64

CHAPTER 1

OOUCH! My Tooth Hurts

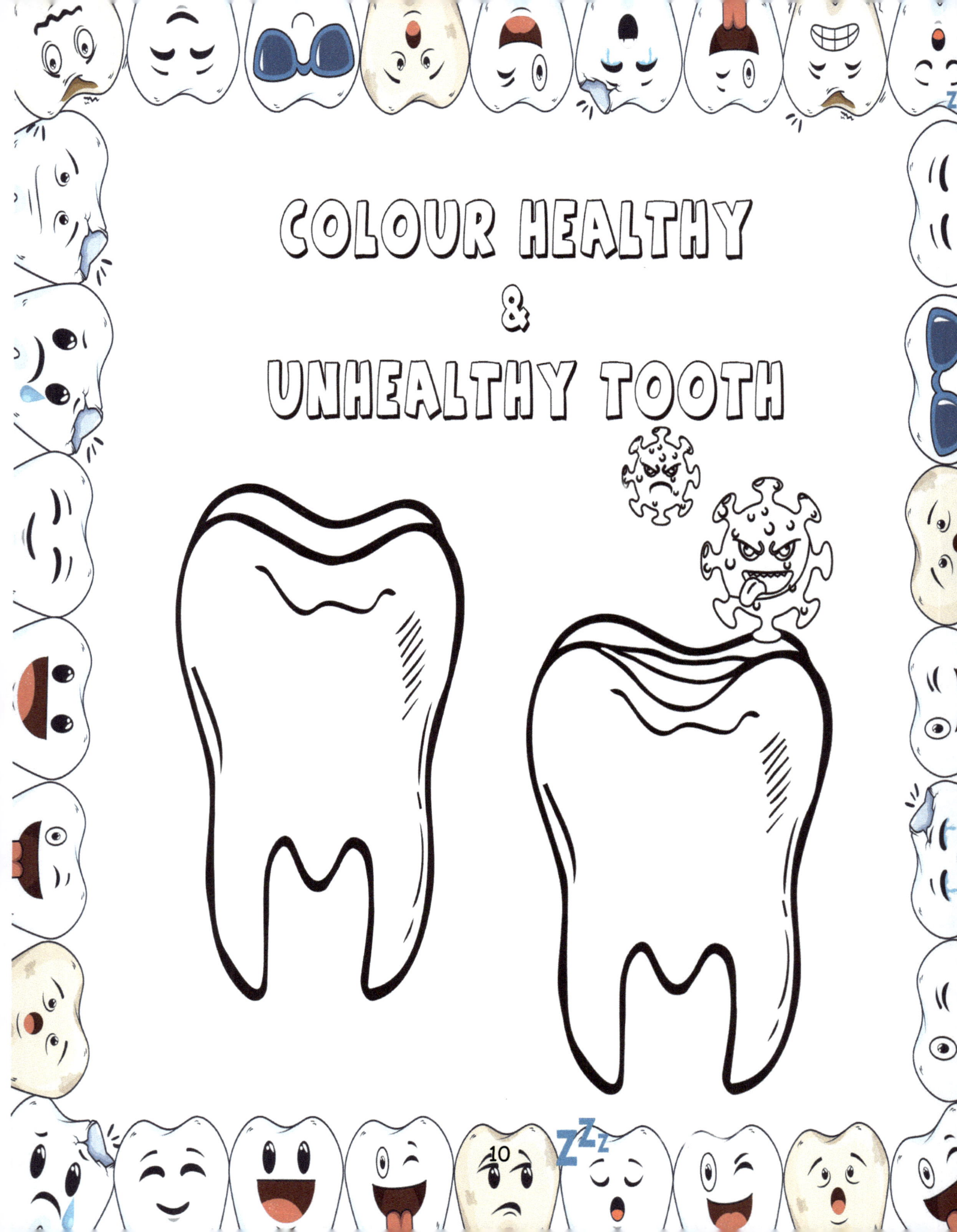

CHAPTER 2

My 1st visit to a Dentist

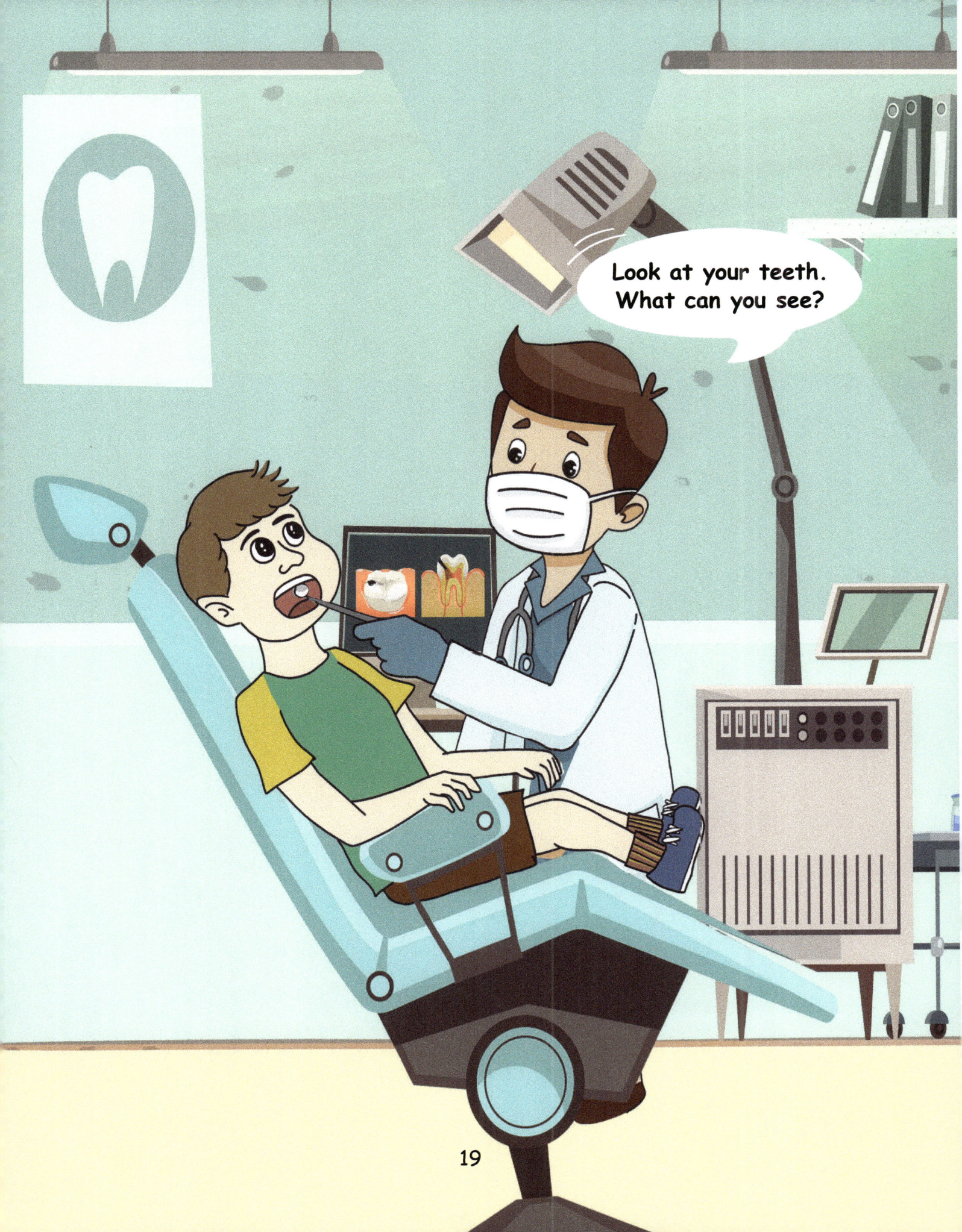

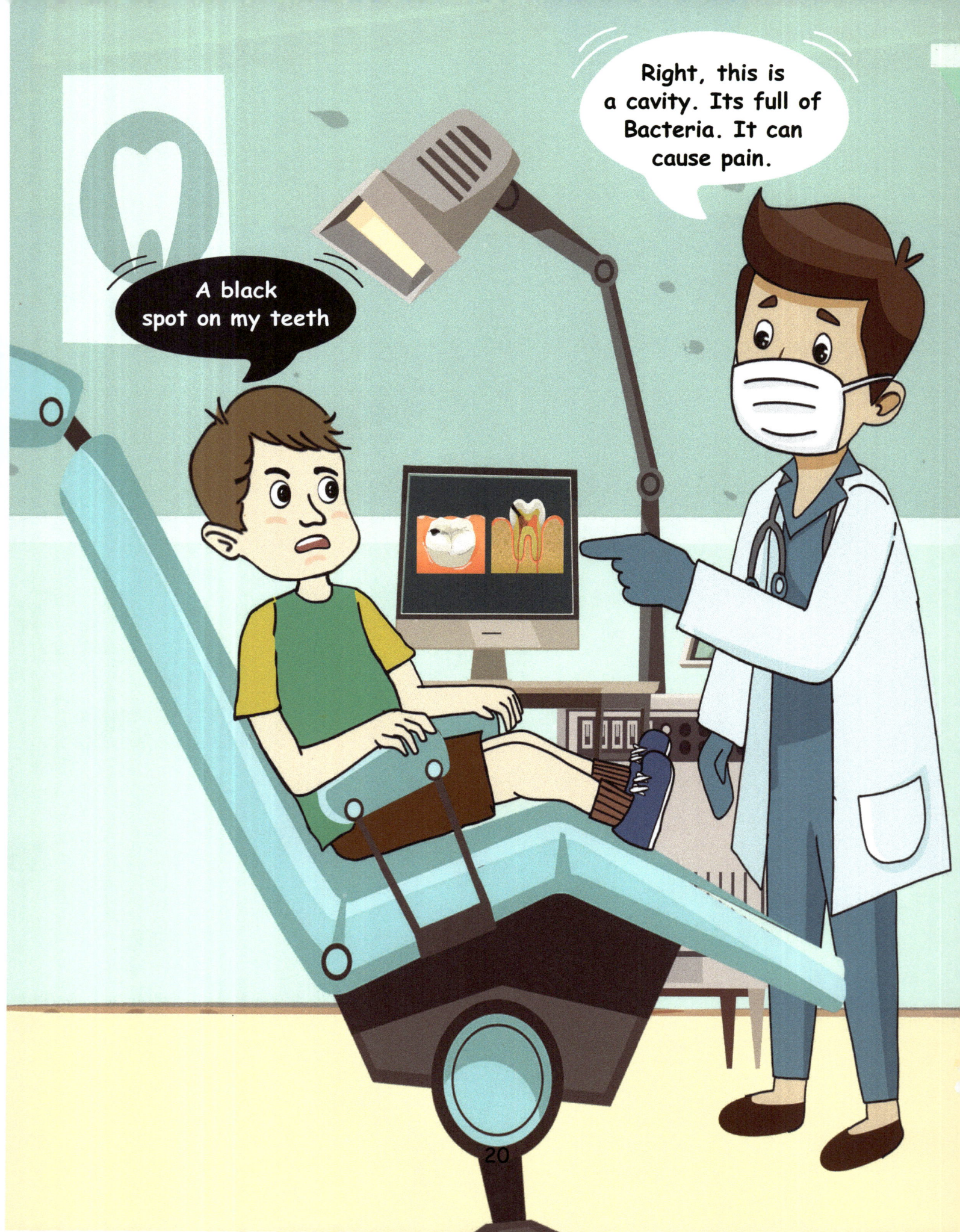

JOIN THE DOTS TO MAKE A DENTAL CHAIR

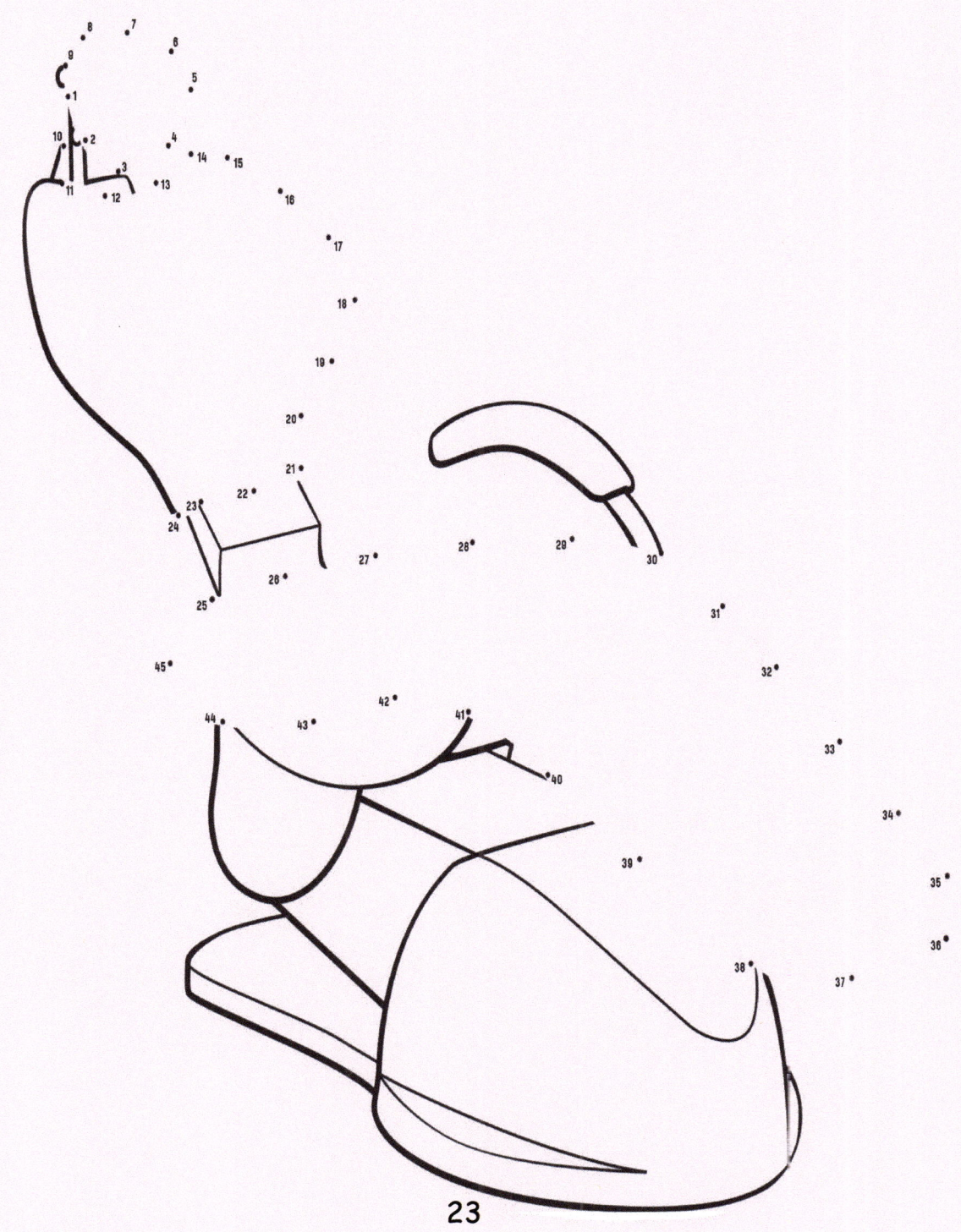

CHAPTER 3

The Treatment begins for a Healthy tooth

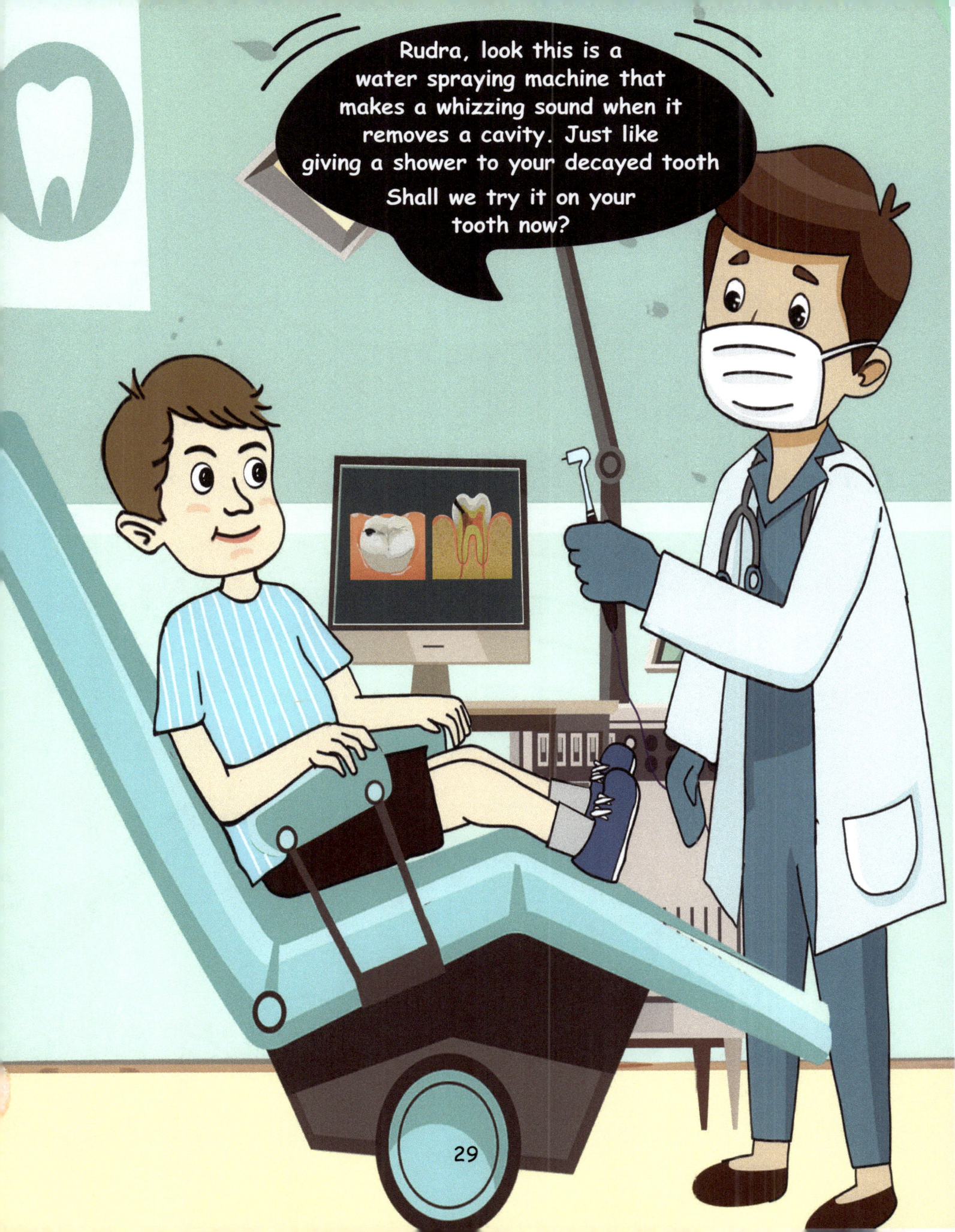

Circle the food good for teeth

CHAPTER 4

Time for a Varnish

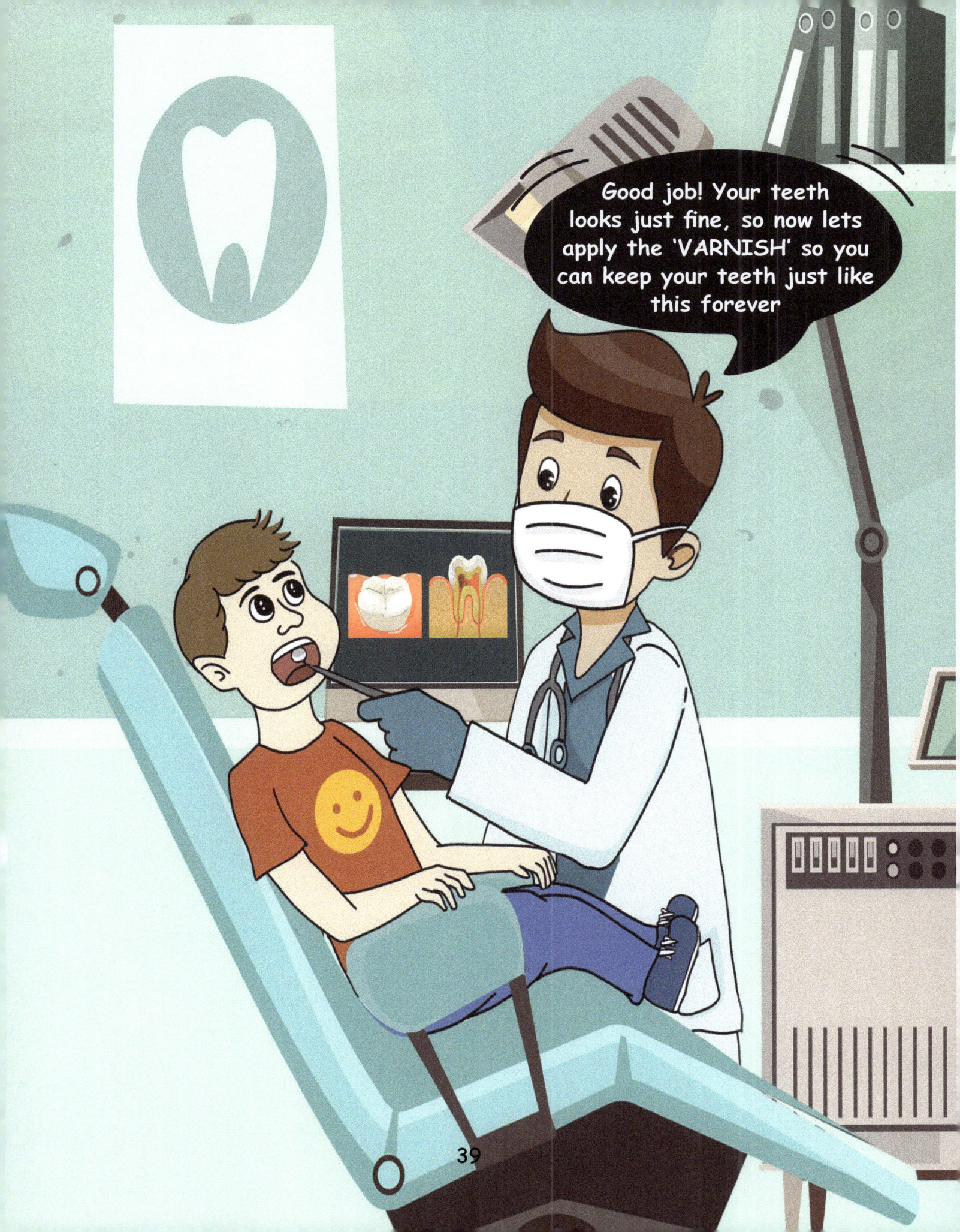

Mom: What is a Varnish?

Dentist: Its a fluoride which helps to strengthen the teeth.

Mom: What is the right age for varnish application?

Dentist: From the time a tooth appears in mouth till 15years of age. Nowadays adults also get it done due to change of food habits.

Mom: How long is treatment time?

Dentist: It takes less than 5 mins, it comes in different flavours.

Mom: Any after care?

Dentist: The child should not eat for few hours preferably for longer results approx. 2-3hours if possible.

Mom: How frequent should it be done?

Dentist: It can be repeated twice a year.

Mom: Any side effects?

Dentist: No side effects

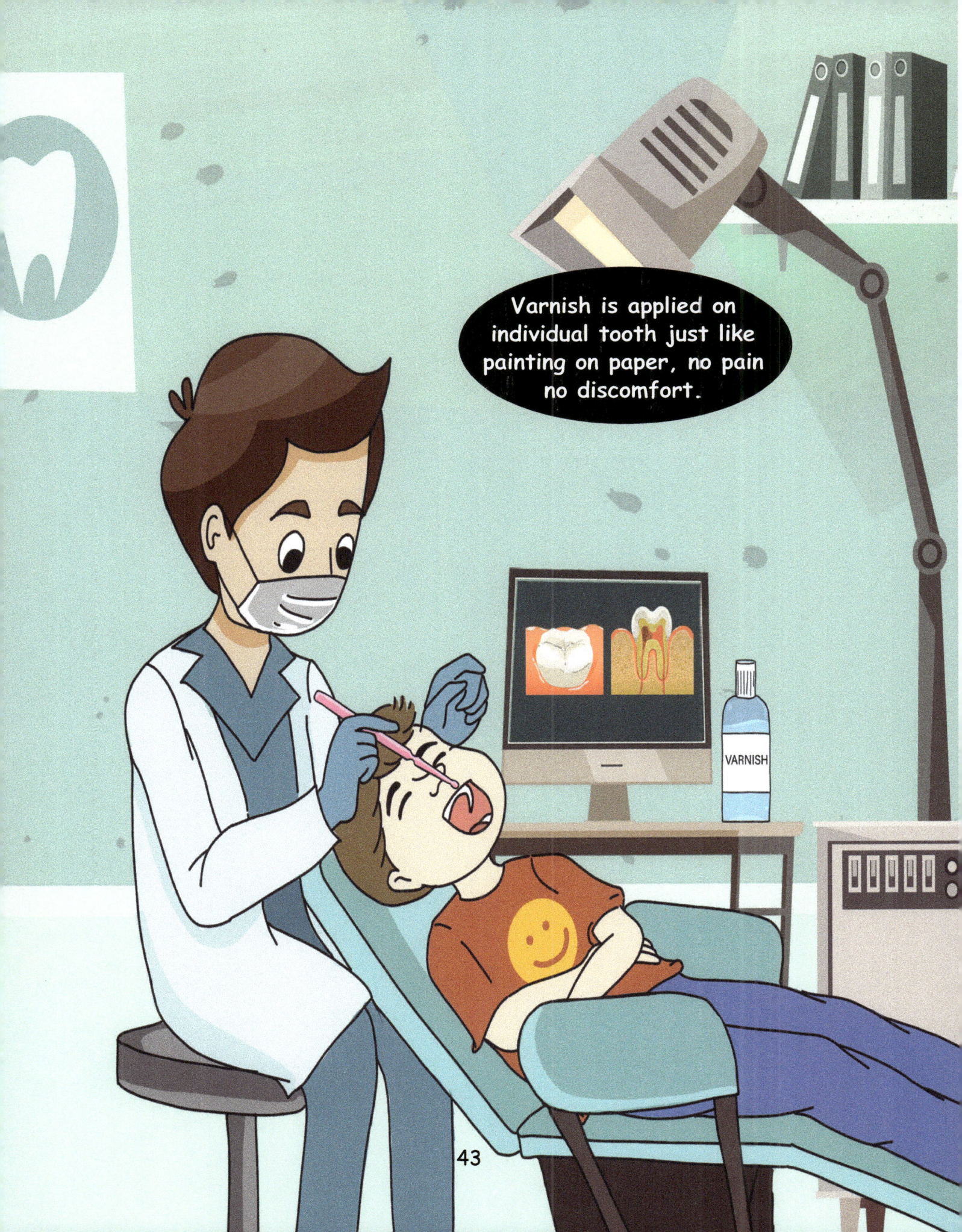

HELP RUDRA REACH FLUORIDE VARNISH !

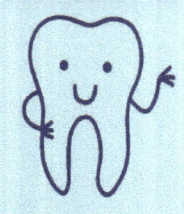
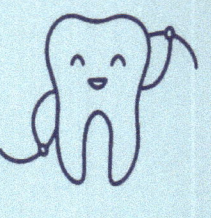

CHAPTER 5

A Wobbly Tooth

The kids teeth time table

Milk teeth (Mean average age)

Lower		Upper
8-13 months	 INCISOR	10-11 months
20 months	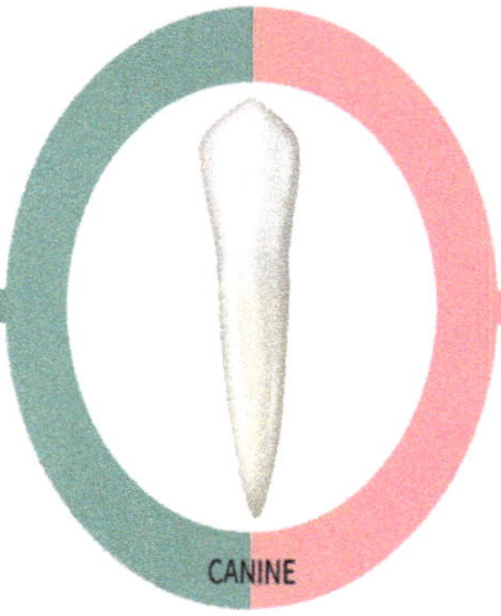 CANINE	19 months
16-27 months	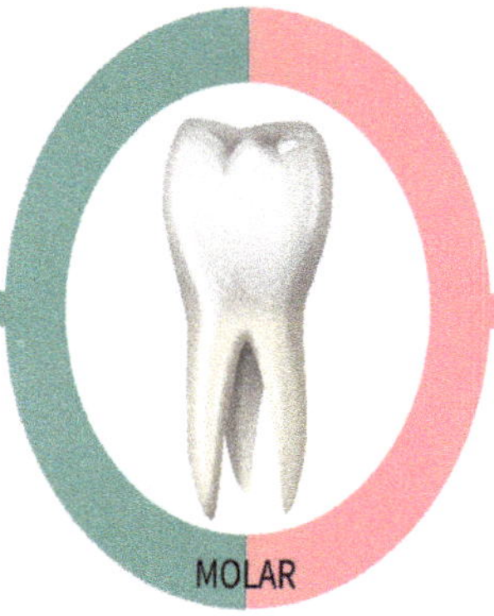 MOLAR	16-29 months

The kids teeth time table

Permanent teeth (Mean average age)

Lower	Tooth	Upper
6-8 years	INCISOR	7-9 years
9-10 years	CANINE	11-12 years
10-12 years	PREMOLAR	10-12 years
6-7 years	1st MOLAR	6-7 years
11-13 years	2nd MOLAR	12-13 years

MATCH TOOTH AND THEIR FUNCTION

INCISOR   CHEWING

CANINE   ASSIST IN CHEWING

PREMOLARS   TEARING

MOLARS   CUTTING

FIND THE FOLLOWING THINGS IN DENTAL CLINIC

(Dental chair, Dentist, kid on chair, mouth mirror, x ray, floss)

CHAPTER 6

Braces for Kids

Fun with Stickers

www.ingramcontent.com/pod-product-compliance
Lightning Source LLC
LaVergne TN
LVHW070539070526
838199LV00076B/6812